Vocabulary Tests
Level 4

Suitable for ages 10 – 12

Each word study unit contains

- Definition matching
- Cloze sentences

Contents		Solutions	
Unit 1	page 2	Unit 1	page 42
Unit 2	page 4	Unit 2	page 42
Unit 3	page 6	Unit 3	page 42
Unit 4	page 8	Unit 4	page 43
Unit 5	page 10	Unit 5	page 43
Unit 6	page 12	Unit 6	page 44
Unit 7	page 14	Unit 7	page 44
Unit 8	page 16	Unit 8	page 44
Unit 9	page 18	Unit 9	page 45
Unit 10	page 20	Unit 10	page 45
Test 1	page 22	Test 1	page 46
Test 2	page 26	Test 2	page 47
Test 3	page 30	Test 3	page 48
Test 4	page 34	Test 4	page 49
Test 5	page 38	Test 5	page 50

Copyright © 2017 Simon Steggels
All rights reserved

No part of this book may be reproduced, stored in a retrieval system, communicated or transmitted in any form or by any means without prior written permission. All inquiries should be made to the publisher.

ISBN 978-0-6480967-8-8

Published by
Advanced Instruction Pty Ltd
www.advancedinstruction.com.au

Unit 1

Definitions—match the words in the bold with their meanings below

fuse	grant	ballistic	fantasy
skeptical	humbly	experimental	trilogy
welded	venture	riot	entranced
discarded	disheartened	retrieve	foe

1. a string connected to an explosive product that causes it to explode after a length of time; to join together _____
2. a series of three books, plays, etc. written about the same situation or characters, forming a continuous story _____
3. lost confidence, hope, and energy _____
4. a story or genre about situations that are very different from real life, usually involving magic _____
5. relating to tests, especially scientific ones _____
6. joined two pieces of metal together permanently by melting _____
7. a noisy, violent, and uncontrolled public gathering _____
8. in a way that shows that you do not think you are important _____
9. doubting that something is true or useful _____
10. to find and bring back something _____
11. to risk going somewhere or doing something that might be dangerous or unpleasant _____
12. threw something away; no longer wanted or needed _____
13. very angry _____
14. to give or allow, usually in an official way; an amount of money to be used for study or research _____
15. cannot stop watching something or someone; captivated _____
16. an enemy _____

Unit 1

Word usage—complete the sentences using the words in bold from the previous page

1. The famous series of books is being made into a movie _____.

2. I prefer to read _____ rather than factual books.

3. If your dad finds out you've been skipping school, he'll go _____.

4. Computers are used to store and _____ information efficiently.

5. The government fears that a _____ will break out as more stores run out of food and water.

6. The drug for treating cancer is still at the _____ stage.

7. The children sat silently on the carpet, _____ by the puppet show.

8. She was _____ by her poor results in English as she had worked hard.

9. The two countries have declared war against their common _____.

10. He _____ accepted his award for helping others.

11. She was given a _____ to study abroad for one year.

12. _____ food containers and bottles littered the streets.

13. Iron spikes have been _____ to the railings around the embassy.

14. I will rarely _____ outside, except when I have to stock up on food.

15. Many experts remain _____ of his claims about finding gold.

16. He lit the _____ on the rocket and ran for cover.

© MR STEGGELS ADVANCED INSTRUCTION PTY LTD

Unit 2

Definitions—match the words in the bold with their meanings below

extravagant	**summon**	**fusion**	**insurance**
brooding	**petrified**	**organic**	**fictitious**
ambassador	**cross**	**debris**	**modern**
light-hearted	**membership**	**barren**	**depicted**

1. annoyed by someone not doing or saying what you want _____
2. broken or torn pieces of something larger _____
3. extremely frightened; frozen to the spot in fear _____
4. not creating or producing anything new, empty of life _____
5. to increase your courage or strength, with great effort _____
6. a chemical substance containing carbon; natural _____
7. happy and not serious _____
8. an agreement in which you pay a company money and they pay your costs if you have an accident, injury _____
9. spending too much money, or using too much of something _____
10. relating to the present or recent times _____
11. when two or more things join or are combined _____
12. represented something in a picture or story _____
13. sad, worried, or angry for a long time _____
14. invented, untrue, not existing _____
15. the state of belonging to an organisation or club _____
16. an important official who works in a foreign country representing his or her own country _____

Unit 2

Word usage—complete the sentences using the words in bold from the previous page

1. I need to register my new car and buy _____ before I can drive it.

2. It took me ages to _____ up the courage to dive into the cold water.

3. He rarely used taxis, which he regarded as _____.

4. My novel is _____ with people and events that are entirely made up.

5. The French _____ was summoned to the Foreign Office.

6. He stood in the corner of the room _____, and refused to dance.

7. You will have to apply for _____ to the golf club before you can play.

8. Our class had a _____ discussion about our holidays.

9. The Sun generates its energy by nuclear _____ of hydrogen into helium.

10. _____ from the tornado was scattered over a large area.

11. I was _____ as the huge dog came bounding up to me.

12. _____ matter comes from organisms that were once alive.

13. My manager became very _____ with me when I did not complete my work for the third week in a row.

14. We drove through a _____ rocky landscape on our way to the volcano.

15. Popart artists are most interested in _____ culture and products.

16. Many famous artists have _____ religious scenes in their artworks.

Unit 3

Definitions—match the words in the bold with their meanings below

snorkeling	joint	exquisite	squabble
boogie board	baste	beloved	disagreement
doubled over	strenuous	vile	paltry
befriended	sermon	enchanting	bitter

1. a large piece of meat that is cooked in one piece _____
2. extremely unpleasant _____
3. swimming while using a tube that you hold in your mouth to help you breathe with your face underwater _____
4. loved very much _____
5. very beautiful and delicate _____
6. a short, light board that you lie on and ride over waves; the act of riding on such a board _____
7. very pleasant _____
8. were friendly towards someone _____
9. a situation in which people do not have the same opinion _____
10. to pour hot fat and liquid over meat while it is cooking _____
11. needing or using a lot of physical or mental effort or energy _____
12. angry, unhappy; unable to forget bad things that happened _____
13. a part of a Christian church ceremony in which a priest gives a talk on a religious or moral subject _____
14. very small and of little or no value _____
15. an argument over something that is not important _____
16. suddenly bend forwards and down, usually because of pain or laughter _____

© MR STEGGELS ADVANCED INSTRUCTION PTY LTD

Unit 3

Word usage—complete the sentences using the words in bold from the previous page

1. She had suffered misfortune over the years but it hadn't made her _____.

2. The builder and I had a _____ about the work he did on my house.

3. Most of the crowd was _____ with laughter at the comedian's jokes.

4. The twins always _____ over who is going to hold the dog's lead.

5. The company offered me a _____ raise, which I reluctantly accepted.

6. St Marta is described in the guidebook as "an _____ medieval city".

7. My family enjoyed _____ on the Great Barrier Reef.

8. The stray dog was _____ by an old lady, who took him in and fed him.

9. I enjoy riding my _____ at the beach; it is safer than a surfboard.

10. Following his operation, he was not allowed to do any _____ exercise.

11. Today's _____ at church was on the importance of compassion.

12. The chef bought a pork _____ to slow roast over the coals.

13. I recently purchased an _____ Chinese vase for $500.

14. It is important to _____ the turkey at regular intervals.

15. He was a gifted teacher _____ by all those he had taught.

16. My little brother has a _____ temper when he doesn't get enough sleep.

© MR STEGGELS ADVANCED INSTRUCTION PTY LTD

Unit 4

Definitions—match the words in the bold with their meanings below

immense	characteristics	culprit	manufactured
surrender	specific	services	system
conditions	herding	scrapheap	activate
rejected	sturdy	reckon	emission

1. moving a group of animals together to another place
2. describes the environment in which something happens or exists
3. particular qualities that are typical of someone or something
4. to declare that you have been defeated and will stop fighting
5. strong and not easily hurt or affected by what happens
6. believe that something is true
7. to make a piece of equipment or a process start working
8. someone who is responsible for doing something bad
9. extremely large
10. made goods in large quantities in a factory
11. did not agree to an offer, proposal, or request
12. a substance, especially a gas, released into the air
13. a set of connected things that work together for a purpose
14. involving only one particular thing or type of thing
15. a pile of articles no longer wanted or needed, especially metal
16. work or duties done for a person or an organisation

Unit 4

Word usage—complete the sentences using the words in bold from the previous page

1. Business analysts _____ their profits have fallen by around 10%.

2. An _____ amount of money has already been spent on the project.

3. The factory workers were thrown on the _____ at the age of fifty.

4. The volunteer organisation provides important _____ to people with disabilities in our community.

5. I auditioned for the singing competition but was _____.

6. Rebel forces will finally _____ after three years of bitter fighting.

7. In the future, parents will choose the physical _____ of their children before they are even born.

8. He has _____ legs which is why he is very good at weightlifting.

9. You must enter the digits in a _____ order or the safe will not open.

10. If _____ in this hospital don't improve, it may have to be closed because of health concerns.

11. Every summer I work on my uncle's farm, _____ sheep.

12. Detectives have so far failed to find the _____ responsible for spraying graffiti all over our wall.

13. I installed a security _____ after my shop was burgled twice.

14. The _____ of greenhouse gases is a problem for our planet.

15. You can _____ the doors by using voice or facial recognition.

16. The clothing company _____ clothes for infants.

© MR STEGGELS ADVANCED INSTRUCTION PTY LTD

Unit 5

Definitions—match the words in the bold with their meanings below

flock	**formula**	**electronics**	**mode**
belfry	**military**	**technology**	**maiden voyage**
toppling	**scientifically**	**animation**	**hovercraft**
anonymous	**compact**	**market**	**fantasies**

1. moving images created from drawings, models that are photographed or created by a computer _____
2. by someone whose name is not known or not made public _____
3. the tower of a church where bells are hung _____
4. the people who might want to buy something, a part of the economy where products and services are sold _____
5. to move or come together in large numbers; a large number of animals _____
6. machinery and devices developed from scientific knowledge _____
7. a way of operating, living, or behaving; a type of something _____
8. losing balance and falling over _____
9. the first journey made by a ship, aircraft or other craft _____
10. in a way that uses the organised methods of science _____
11. relating to or belonging to the armed forces _____
12. a vehicle that travels quickly just above the surface of water or land by producing a current of air under it to support it _____
13. consisting of parts that are positioned closely or in a tidy way, using very little space _____
14. a standard way of doing or making something; can be a secret _____
15. pleasant situations that you enjoy thinking about but which are unlikely to happen _____
16. the scientific study of electric current and technology _____

Unit 5

Word usage—complete the sentences using the words in bold from the previous page

1. Railways are an important _____ of transport for the economy.

2. One of my _____ is to drive a super-charged V8 racing car.

3. The _____ sped across the harbour on its way to the seaside resort.

4. The HMS Titanic sank, after hitting an iceberg on its _____.

5. Are you sure there's a _____ for broccoli ice cream? It sounds awful.

6. Organisers are expecting many people to _____ to the free concert.

7. An _____ caller had given police a tip-off about the robbery.

8. Due to advances in computer _____ software, it is now possible to make cartoons much more quickly than in the past.

9. Each Sunday, I have to climb to the _____ to ring the church bells.

10. This medicine is _____ proven to reduce cholesterol.

11. The soldiers had to wear _____ uniform for the presentation ceremony.

12. What a _____ apartment! How did you fit so much into so little space?

13. Modern _____ allows us to communicate with each other over vast distances, almost immediately.

14. He is studying _____ as he wants to become an electrical engineer.

15. There is no magic _____ for success in business.

16. Because it had been built on sand, the building was at risk of _____ over.

© MR STEGGELS ADVANCED INSTRUCTION PTY LTD

Unit 6

Definitions—match the words in the bold with their meanings below

pig-headed	peril	paternal	built-in
texture	unruly	maternal	hieroglyphs
routine	melodic	arduous	truncated
mirage	pace	heir	nuisance

1. great danger, or something that is very dangerous _____
2. a usual or fixed way of doing things _____
3. of or like a father _____
4. showing unreasonable support for an opinion or plan of action and refusing to change or listen to different opinions _____
5. involving great effort; difficult and tiring _____
6. difficult to keep tidy neat, often sticking up or out _____
7. the degree to which something is rough, smooth, soft or hard _____
8. permanently connected and cannot be easily removed _____
9. a person who receives money, or property, especially a member of the same family, when that other person dies _____
10. related to a mother's side of the family _____
11. the speed at which someone or something moves, or with which something happens or changes _____
12. made briefer or shorter, usually by removing a part _____
13. pictures or symbols that represent a word, used in some writing systems, such as the one used in ancient Egypt _____
14. very pleasant to listen to _____
15. something or someone that annoys you or causes trouble _____
16. an image, produced by very hot air, of something that seems to be far away but does not really exist _____

Unit 6

Word usage—complete the sentences using the words in bold from the previous page

1. All of the bedrooms in this apartment have _____ wardrobes.

2. Despite having a large family, the King and Queen had no son and _____.

3. Traveling long distances by horse-drawn coach would have been _____.

4. In the middle of winter, summer seems like a distant _____.

5. The _____ man would not leave his desk even as the building was being evacuated and smoke was filling the corridors.

6. This artificial fabric has the _____ of cotton.

7. The child's singing voice was unexpectedly _____.

8. Uncle Michael is very _____ with his baby niece.

9. There is no fixed _____ in our classroom - every day is different.

10. My _____ grandmother is sick so my mother is worried.

11. The boy tried to comb his _____ mop of black hair.

12. The _____ story fit into the magazine but the ending had been left out.

13. The narrow ledge began to crumble, placing the hikers in _____.

14. I thought I heard someone following me, so I quickened my _____.

15. The symbols on the cave wall were nothing like Egyptian _____.

16. Local residents claimed that the noise from the bar was a _____.

Unit 7

Definitions—match the words in the bold with their meanings below

ratio	**anticipated**	**riband**	**taunting**
survey	**hair-raising**	**crockery**	**frail**
affect	**cinematography**	**rash**	**measured**
occurrence	**tension**	**jackdaw**	**conditioned**

1. careless or unwise, without thought for what might happen _____

2. an examination of opinions made by asking people questions _____

3. a ribbon, especially one used as a decoration _____

4. very frightening _____

5. the relationship between two groups or amounts that expresses how much bigger one is than the other _____

6. mental or emotional strain _____

7. the fact of something existing, or how much of it exists _____

8. cups, plates, bowls, used to serve food and drink _____

9. the art and methods of film photography _____

10. weak or unhealthy, or easily damaged, broken, or harmed _____

11. to have an influence on someone or something, or to cause a change in someone or something _____

12. imagined or expected that something will happen _____

13. trained or influenced someone so that they act in a certain way without thinking about it _____

14. careful and controlled _____

15. intentionally upsetting someone by making unkind remarks or laughing unkindly _____

16. a black and grey bird of the crow family, known for taking bright objects back to its nest _____

Unit 7

Word usage—complete the sentences using the words in bold from the previous page

1. The parent responded in a calm and _____ way when the toddler began screaming for a new toy.

2. The _____ of boys to girls in the class was two to one.

3. Boys are _____ not to cry as it is seen as a weakness in males.

4. The fire will _____ neighbouring buildings if it is not contained.

5. I hadn't seen my grandfather for a month and was surprised by how _____ and old he looked.

6. A recent _____ revealed that obesity rates in children are on the rise.

7. A _____ has been stealing the colourful pegs from our clothesline.

8. She gave a _____ account of her escape from a bear while hiking.

9. I could feel the _____ in the room as we waited for our exam results.

10. The film about Antarctica was tipped to win the Oscar for Best _____.

11. This study compares the _____ of cancer in various countries.

12. It was a _____ decision - he didn't think about the consequences.

13. The winner of the race was presented with a special _____.

14. Greeks often smash plaster _____ during celebrations.

15. We had not _____ two flat tyres on our camping trip.

16. Bullies enjoy _____ people as it makes them feel more powerful.

© MR STEGGELS ADVANCED INSTRUCTION PTY LTD

Unit 8

Definitions—match the words in the bold with their meanings below

superstitious	**boycott**	**apprentice**	**applicant**
prop	**intend**	**anatomy**	**perceptions**
quiche	**issue**	**representation**	**robust**
clover	**refreshments**	**canal**	**critical**

1. someone who works for a skilled person in order to learn that person's skills _____

2. to have as a plan or purpose _____

3. small amounts of food and drink _____

4. to support something by leaning it against something else or putting something under it; an item used in a performance _____

5. to refuse to buy a product or take part in an activity as a way of expressing strong disapproval _____

6. the scientific study of the body and how its parts are arranged _____

7. a small green plant with three round leaves on each stem _____

8. a long, thin stretch of water that is artificially made for boats to travel along _____

9. a subject that people are thinking and talking about _____

10. expressing negative comments or judgments _____

11. the way that someone or something is shown or described _____

12. describes someone who believes that causes for events are based old ideas about magic _____

13. beliefs or opinions, often held by many people and based on how things seem _____

14. a person who applies for something, especially a job _____

15. strong and healthy; unlikely to break or fail _____

16. an open pastry case, filled with a mixture of eggs, cream, and other savoury foods, that is baked _____

© MR STEGGELS ADVANCED INSTRUCTION PTY LTD

Unit 8

Word usage—complete the sentences using the words in bold from the previous page

1. We _____ to travel to Europe next year, for a three-week holiday.

2. Light _____ were available at the back of the hall.

3. The window will not stay open—please _____ it open.

4. A detailed understanding of human _____ is important to a doctor.

5. Some people are _____ about black cats crossing their path.

6. The photocopier is a _____ piece of machinery that has never broken down or needed repair.

7. The Panama _____ provides a crucial shipping link between the Atlantic Ocean and the Pacific Ocean.

8. His photographs of Afghanistan will change people's _____ of the country and its people.

9. The art lecture was about the _____ of cats in Ancient Egyptian art.

10. People were urged to _____ the country's products because of its terrible treatment of the environment.

11. My father is _____ of my handwriting; he says that it is messy.

12. Most of the work on our renovation was done by an _____.

13. The students raised the _____ of bullying, at the council meeting.

14. I made a beautiful ham and cheese _____ with salad, for lunch.

15. Many people believe that a four-leafed _____ will bring good luck.

16. Is there another _____ for this job, or am I the only one?

Unit 9

Definitions—match the words in the bold with their meanings below

groundbreaking	stern	drone	traditional
benefits	furrowed	contorted	introduced
careering	exotic	condemned	migrants
imitation	separation	shimmered	homeland

1. unusual and interesting, especially something foreign _____

2. making new discoveries, using new methods and tools _____

3. being part of the unchanging customs of a group of people or ways of behaving _____

4. advantages, improvements, or help _____

5. shone with a soft light, shaking slightly _____

6. the division of something into its distinct elements _____

7. moving quickly in an out-of-control way _____

8. skin on the face formed deep lines or folds, especially because of worry or concentration _____

9. a copy of something _____

10. people who go to live in another area or country, especially in order to find work _____

11. brought a type of thing somewhere for the first time; put into a new environment _____

12. serious and strict, and showing strong disapproval _____

13. twisted or bent in an unnatural way _____

14. the country where someone was born _____

15. disapproved of completely; sentenced to death _____

16. a continuous low dull sound _____

Unit 9

Word usage—complete the sentences using the words in bold from the previous page

1. The _____ from the exhaust fan kept me awake all night.

2. Crushed ore is mixed with cyanide to achieve a _____ of up to 96 percent pure gold.

3. Thanks to _____ research, scientists found a cure for the disease.

4. 'Put your hand up before speaking,' said my teacher, in a _____ voice.

5. The students were beginning to reap the _____ of all their hard work.

6. When he came to the harder problems, his brow _____ in concentration.

7. She wore an _____ fur coat to the opera.

8. At the zoo, there was a special enclosure for _____ birds.

9. The convicted smugglers were _____ to death.

10. His face _____ in terror as a ghost appeared in the doorway.

11. My toboggan went _____ down the slope so I dived off to save myself.

12. The surface of the lake _____ in the moonlight.

13. The New Year celebrations featured _____ dances and food.

14. The chef _____ a new range of healthy food for children.

15. A lot of factory work is done by _____ who don't speak English well.

16. Many people are forced to flea their _____ because of war and famine.

© MR STEGGELS ADVANCED INSTRUCTION PTY LTD

Unit 10

Definitions—match the words in the bold with their meanings below

stringent	shrill	shuttle	truancy
genuine	extinguish	threadbare	reviewer
prominent	whereabouts	breastplate	praised
inflame	potential	heroic	amnesty

1. a piece of armour that protects the chest _____
2. real and exactly what it appears to be _____
3. clothes have become thin or damaged _____
4. strict, precise conditions or requirements _____
5. to travel regularly between two places; a vehicle used for this purpose _____
6. to intensify feelings, especially anger; to make a situation worse _____
7. being absent from school regularly without permission _____
8. very brave or great _____
9. possible when the necessary conditions exist _____
10. someone who writes their opinion of a book, play, film etc _____
11. having a loud and high sound that is unpleasant to listen to _____
12. a decision by a government to free political prisoners _____
13. the location of a person or thing _____
14. stop a fire burning _____
15. expressed admiration or approval about the achievements or characteristics of a person or thing _____
16. important, well-known, noticeable _____

Unit 10

Word usage—complete the sentences using the words in bold from the previous page

1. The political activist was freed under the terms of the _____.

2. My parents _____ me when I did well at school.

3. The criminal escaped from jail; his exact _____ is a mystery.

4. If this is a _____ Michelangelo drawing, it will sell for millions.

5. The _____ wrote that he did not like the new *Revengers* movie.

6. The fire safety regulations for the new high-rise building were very _____.

7. _____ is a big problem for schools in city areas.

8. Rescuing the family from their burning house was a _____ deed.

9. My sister has a _____, high-pitched voice that is quite annoying.

10. The knight wore a _____ of pure silver.

11. A bus is used to _____ passengers between the domestic terminal, international terminal and the car park.

12. Unfortunately, the President's comments will _____ the situation further and lead to more violent protests and arrests.

13. Many _____ customers are waiting for the yearly sale before buying.

14. The man wore a _____ coat that did not protect him against the cold.

15. He was a _____ member of the Architects' Guild.

16. It took several hours for firefighters to _____ the blaze.

Test 1

1. Which word means **a way of operating, living, or behaving; a type of something**?

    A   formula
    B   mode
    C   routine
    D   technology

2. Choose the best meaning of the word **entranced**

    A   cannot stop watching something or someone; captivated
    B   happy and not serious
    C   extremely frightened
    D   losing balance and falling over

3. Choose the word that is closest in meaning to **stern**

    A   robust
    B   unruly
    C   stringent
    D   critical

4. Choose the word that is most opposite in meaning to **inflame**

    A   baste
    B   surrender
    C   fuse
    D   extinguish

5. Which is the odd word out?

    A   ambassador
    B   reviewer
    C   applicant
    D   apprentice

© MR STEGGELS ADVANCED INSTRUCTION PTY LTD

6. Choose the word that best completes the sentence

    Species that are _____ into an ecosystem often have no natural predators.

    A   petrified
    B   introduced
    C   welded
    D   befriended

7. The letters in **mmnosu** can be rearranged to make a word meaning

    A   sad, worried, or angry for a long time
    B   to believe that something is true
    C   a priest's speech on a religious or moral subject
    D   to increase your courage or strength, with great effort

8. Which pair of words is closest in meaning?

    A   squabble   disagreement
    B   humbly   unruly
    C   discarded   depicted
    D   occurrence conditions

9. Which pair of words is most opposite in meaning?

    A   animation   cinematography
    B   welded   fuse
    C   hair-raising barren
    D   imitation   genuine

10. Which word should replace the words in bold in the following sentence?

    I **suddenly bend forwards and down because of laughter** when my friend fell victim to my practical joke.

    A   taunting
    B   doubled over
    C   contorted
    D   truncated

11. Which is green in colour?

    A   clover
    B   jackdaw
    C   belfry
    D   none of the above

12. A **survey** is also called

    A   an issue
    B   a representation
    C   an examination
    D   an amnesty

13. Someone who is **pig-headed** can best be described as

    A   stubborn
    B   vile
    C   unruly
    D   a nuisance

14. Which is related to the sense of touch?

    A   bitter
    B   texture
    C   emission
    D   mirage

15. Which is the odd word out?

    A   reckon
    B   baste
    C   prop
    D   foe

© MR STEGGELS ADVANCED INSTRUCTION PTY LTD

16. Choose the word that best completes the sentence

    For security reasons, the _____ of pop singer Bustin Jeiber remain secret.

    A   perceptions
    B   services
    C   whereabouts
    D   none of the above

17. The letters in **odern** can be rearranged to make a word meaning

    A   a continuous low dull sound
    B   a copy of something
    C   a decision by a government to free political prisoners
    D   none of the above

18. Which pair of words is closest in meaning?

    A   arduous   strenuous
    B   riot   boycott
    C   intend   potential
    D   brooding   enchanting

19. Choose the best definition of the word **tension**

    A   strong and healthy; unlikely to break or fail
    B   expressing negative comments or judgments
    C   careful and controlled
    D   mental or emotional strain

20. Which word should replace the words in bold in the following sentence?

    We all **imagined or expected** an exciting performance as the lights went down in the auditorium and the curtains opened.

    A   expedition
    B   destination
    C   anticipated
    D   route

Test 2

1. Which word means **lost confidence, hope, and energy**?

    A   discarded
    B   disheartened
    C   frail
    D   scrapheap

2. Choose the best meaning of the word **insurance**

    A   to make a piece of equipment or a process start working
    B   the state of belonging to an organisation or club
    C   spending too much money, or using too much of something
    D   an agreement in which a company pays your costs if you have an accident

3. Choose the word that is closest in meaning to **sturdy**

    A   riot
    B   robust
    C   rash
    D   heroic

4. Choose the word that is most opposite in meaning to **organic**

    A   compact
    B   quiche
    C   debris
    D   manufactured

5. Which is associated with cattle?

    A   snorkeling
    B   hair-raising
    C   brooding
    D   herding

© MR STEGGELS ADVANCED INSTRUCTION PTY LTD

6. Choose the word that best completes the sentence

   Customers threatened to _____ the company until it could prove that its products had not been tested on animals.

   A   boycott
   B   inflame
   C   discard
   D   retrieve

7. The letters in **tinned** can be rearranged to make a word meaning

   A   expressing negative comments or judgments
   B   beliefs or opinions, often held by many people and based on how things seem
   C   the way that someone or something is shown or described
   D   to have as a plan or purpose

8. Which pair of words is closest in meaning?

   A   paltry   frail
   B   nuisance   unruly
   C   toppling   sturdy
   D   rejected   discarded

9. Which pair of words is most opposite in meaning?

   A   petrified   shimmered
   B   fusion   separation
   C   conditions   characteristics
   D   depicted   representation

10. Which word should replace the words in bold in the following sentence?

    Members of the council outlined the many **advantages or improvements** that a new library would bring to the community.

    A   conditions
    B   perceptions
    C   benefits
    D   fantasies

© MR STEGGELS ADVANCED INSTRUCTION PTY LTD

11. Choose the best word to complete the sentence

    Sharon worked as an _____ mechanic for two years before opening her own auto repair shop.

    A   applicant
    B   apprentice
    C   anonymous
    D   arduous

12. Which would you find in a kitchen?

    A   crockery
    B   a jackdaw
    C   a riband
    D   a breastplate

13. Which word means **in a way that uses the organised methods of science**?

    A   technology
    B   scientifically
    C   experimental
    D   none of the above

14. Choose the word that is most similar in meaning to **peril**

    A   ballistic
    B   danger
    C   riot
    D   frail

15. Which is the odd word out?

    A   truancy
    B   amnesty
    C   humbly
    D   cinematography

© MR STEGGELS ADVANCED INSTRUCTION PTY LTD

16. Choose the words that best complete the sentence

    The _____ used advanced _____ to locate enemy forces.

    A   hovercraft   system
    B   military   technology
    C   migrants   cinematography
    D   ambassador   herding

17. The letters in **conker** can be rearranged to make a word meaning

    A   to believe that something is true
    B   someone who is responsible for doing something bad
    C   work or duties done for a person or an organisation
    D   difficult to keep tidy neat, often sticking up or out

18. Which pair of words is most opposite in meaning?

    A   melodic   shrill
    B   threadbare   exotic
    C   skeptical   superstitious
    D   ratio   formula

19. Choose a subject that could be studied

    A   anatomy
    B   cinematography
    C   electronics
    D   all of the above

20. Which word should replace the words in bold in the following sentence?

    Up ahead, I thought I saw a city rising from the desert sand, but it was just **an image created by hot air and did not really exist**.

    A   a mode
    B   a fantasy
    C   a mirage
    D   a perception

Test 3

1. Which word means **doubting that something is true or useful**?

    A   fictitious
    B   superstitious
    C   skeptical
    D   none of the above

2. Choose the best meaning of the word **grant**

    A   to give or allow an amount of money to be used for study or research
    B   relating to tests, especially scientific ones
    C   spending too much money, or using too much of something
    D   annoyed by someone not doing or saying what you want

3. Choose the word that is closest in meaning to **ballistic**

    A   disagreeable
    B   worried
    C   furious
    D   not serious

4. Choose the word that is most opposite in meaning to **anonymous**

    A   unknown
    B   praised
    C   modernist
    D   prominent

5. Which is the odd word out?

    A   activate
    B   baste
    C   ratio
    D   affect

© MR STEGGELS ADVANCED INSTRUCTION PTY LTD

6. Choose the word that best completes the sentence

   Only the bravest of explorers would _____ into uncharted waters.

   A   surrender
   B   maiden voyage
   C   activate
   D   venture

7. The letters in **dweeld** can be rearranged to make a word meaning

   A   a string connected to an explosive product that causes it to explode
   B   joined two pieces of metal together permanently by melting
   C   a noisy, violent, and uncontrolled public gathering
   D   broken or torn pieces of something larger

8. Which word should replace the words in bold in the following sentence?

   He was **spending too much money** every time he shopped for new clothes and accessories.

   A   cross
   B   entranced
   C   extravagant
   D   truncated

9. Choose the best word to complete the sentence

   The council is responsible for providing a range of _____ to the community.

   A   conditions
   B   services
   C   technology
   D   refreshments

10. Which word should replace the words in bold in the following sentence?

    Police are hoping to identify the **person responsible for committing the crime** by using video surveillance footage.

    A   nuisance
    B   whereabouts
    C   foe
    D   culprit

© MR STEGGELS ADVANCED INSTRUCTION PTY LTD

11. Choose the best word to complete the sentence

    _____ to my gym is quite expensive as it has a heated pool and tennis court.

    A   Applicants
    B   Truancy
    C   Membership
    D   Representation

12. Which pair is the most opposite in meaning?

    A   paltry   extravagant
    B   welded   fusion
    C   summon   discarded
    D   venture   riot

13. Which would you most likely find on a **scrapheap**?

    A   debris
    B   hieroglyphs
    C   quiche
    D   discarded

14. What is the best definition of **barren**?

    A   very small and of little or no value
    B   broken or torn pieces of something larger
    C   not creating or producing anything new, empty of life
    D   none of the above

15. Which would be found in an ancient tomb?

    A   emissions
    B   hieroglyphs
    C   fuse
    D   belfry

© MR STEGGELS ADVANCED INSTRUCTION PTY LTD

16. Choose the word that best completes the sentence

    The go-kart went _____ down the embankment toward the river.

    A   hair-raising
    B   doubled over
    C   toppling
    D   careering

17. The letters in **nyuurl** can be rearranged to make a word meaning

    A   permanently connected and cannot be easily removed
    B   difficult to keep tidy neat, often sticking up or out
    C   involving great effort; difficult and tiring
    D   the speed at which someone or something moves

18. Whose job is it to offer a **critical** opinion about a film or play?

    A   an apprentice
    B   a reviewer
    C   an ambassador
    D   a foe

19. Choose the word most opposite in meaning to **retreive**

    A   depict
    B   grant
    C   praise
    D   discard

20. Which word should replace the words in bold in the following sentence?

    I designed a **set of connected things that work together for a purpose** to dispatch mail quickly.

    A   system
    B   formula
    C   routine
    D   ratio

Test 4

1. Which word means **relating to tests, especially scientific ones**?

    A   emission
    B   formula
    C   scientifically
    D   experimental

2. Choose the best meaning of the word **fantasy**

    A   a story about situations that are very different from real life, usually involving magic
    B   the belief that causes for events are based old ideas about magic
    C   to believe that something is true
    D   pleasant situations that you enjoy thinking about but which are unlikely to happen

3. Which word is most opposite in meaning to **enchanting**?

    A   exotic
    B   vile
    C   rejected
    D   brooding

4. Which is most similar in meaning to **twisted**?

    A   beloved
    B   condemned
    C   contorted
    D   truncated

5. Someone who believes that causes for events are based old ideas about magic is

    A   superstitious
    B   light-hearted
    C   entranced
    D   maternal

© MR STEGGELS ADVANCED INSTRUCTION PTY LTD

6. Choose the word that best completes the sentence

   When writing a recipe, it is very important to provide _____ instructions.

   A   ratio
   B   specific
   C   experimental
   D   groundbreaking

7. The letters in **gorilty** can be rearranged to make a word meaning

   A   a story or genre about situations that are very different from real life
   B   a series of three books with the same situations or characters, forming a continuous story
   C   a chemical substance containing carbon; natural
   D   to pour hot fat and liquid over meat while it is cooking

8. Which word should replace the words in bold in the following sentence?

   The general will lead a **planned group of political, business, or military activities** to take control of enemy states by force.

   A   parliament
   B   protest
   C   campaign
   D   none of the above

9. Which of the following can be eaten?

   A   refreshments
   B   joint
   C   quiche
   D   all of the above

10. Which word should replace the words in bold in the following sentence?

    Sisters Jan and Marcia are always **arguing over something that is not important**.

    A   brooding
    B   taunting
    C   squabbling
    D   rioting

11. Choose the words that best complete the following sentence

    _____ down a steep hill on skis is a _____ experience.

A	Toppling	taunting
B	Careering	groundbreaking
C	Careering	hair-raising
D	Toppling	routine

12. Which word is most opposite in meaning to **modern**?

    A   superstition
    B   anticipated
    C   fictitious
    D   traditional

13. Which of the following is mode of transport?

    A   boogie board
    B   hovercraft
    C   maiden voyage
    D   canal

14. Which word should replace the words in bold in the following sentence?

    There was **a standard way** for making his fried chicken that Colonel Flanders wanted kept secret.

    A   a system
    B   a disagreement
    C   insurance
    D   a formula

15. Which word is most opposite to **praised**?

    A   condemned
    B   conditioned
    C   disheartened
    D   beloved

16. Choose the words that best complete the sentence

    Eastville did not agree to the _____ of _____, so Westville decided to end the war by dropping an atomic bomb.

    A   representation   the ambassador
    B   conditions   surrender
    C   characteristics   the venture
    D   perceptions   migrants

17. The letters in **choire** can be rearranged to make a word meaning

    A   very brave or great
    B   important, well-known, noticeable
    C   unusual and interesting, especially something foreign
    D   a group of singers

18. Which would you most likely do on a visit to a coral reef?

    A   boogie board
    B   baste
    C   snorkeling
    D   maiden voyage

19. What is the best meaning for the word **issue**?

    A   an argument or a situation in which people do not have the same opinion
    B   an argument over something that is not important
    C   expressing negative comments or judgments
    D   a subject that people are thinking and talking about

20. Choose the word that best completes the sentence

    In the doughnut recipe, the _____ of flour to sugar is two to one.

    A   formula
    B   characteristics
    C   ratio
    D   potential

© MR STEGGELS ADVANCED INSTRUCTION PTY LTD

Test 5

1. Which word means **represented or shown something in a picture or story**?

    A   supposed
    B   depicted
    C   virtually
    D   insist

2. Choose the best meaning of the word **exquisite**

    A   extremely unpleasant
    B   loved very much
    C   very small and of little or no value
    D   very beautiful and delicate

3. Another word for **truncated** is

    A   permanently connected
    B   controlled
    C   shortened
    D   packaged

4. Choose the word most opposite in meaning to **rash**

    A   measured
    B   genuine
    C   conditioned
    D   petrified

5. Which is the odd word out?

    A   anatomy
    B   military
    C   activate
    D   insurance

© MR STEGGELS ADVANCED INSTRUCTION PTY LTD

6. Choose the words that best complete the sentence

   The _____ escaped their _____ when war broke out.

A	heirs	hovercraft
B	migrants	homeland
C	ambassadors	belfry
D	migrants	amnesty

7. The letters in **etcaff** can be rearranged to make a word meaning

   A   the fact of something existing, or how much of it exists
   B   weak or unhealthy, or easily damaged, broken, or harmed
   C   to have an influence on someone or something, or to cause a change
   D   beliefs or opinions, often held by many people and based on how things seem

8. Which word should replace the words in bold in the following sentence?

   A look of concern **formed deep lines or folds in** my mother's forehead when she learned that I had stolen my brother's pocket money.

   A   contorted
   B   condemned
   C   manufactured
   D   furrowed

9. Choose the best word to complete the sentence

   The designer kitchen featured a _____ butler's pantry with a secret door.

   A   built-in
   B   welded
   C   groundbreaking
   D   prominent

10. What is the meaning of **market**?

    A   to move or come together in large numbers
    B   the part of the economy where products and services are sold
    C   an examination of opinions made by asking people questions
    D   brought a type of thing somewhere for the first time, put into a new environment

© MR STEGGELS ADVANCED INSTRUCTION PTY LTD

11. Which word is both a verb (action) and a noun (a thing)?

    A   baste
    B   immense
    C   flock
    D   riband

12. Choose the word most opposite in meaning to **foe**

    A   beloved
    B   culprit
    C   nuisance
    D   heroic

13. Which word refers to **pleasant situations that you enjoy thinking about but which are unlikely to happen**?

    A   superstitions
    B   mirage
    C   perceptions
    D   fantasies

14. A **canal** is

    A   the first journey made by a ship, aircraft or other craft
    B   a vehicle that travels quickly just above the surface of water or land on a current of air
    C   a long, thin stretch of water that is artificially made for boats to travel along
    D   none of the above

15. Something that is **immense** is not

    A   exquisite
    B   compact
    C   threadbare
    D   toppling

© MR STEGGELS ADVANCED INSTRUCTION PTY LTD

16. Choose the word that best completes the sentence

   The cladding on the tower is a _____ fire hazard and should be removed.

   A   critical
   B   potential
   C   peril
   D   robust

17. The letters in **simonies** can be rearranged to make a word meaning

   A   work or duties done for a person or an organisation
   B   particular qualities that are typical of someone or something
   C   the scientific study of electric current and technology
   D   a substance, especially a gas, released into the air

18. Choose the word most opposite in meaning to **brooding**

   A   light-hearted
   B   hair-raising
   C   humbly
   D   taunting

19. Which word is both a verb (action) and a noun (a thing)?

   A   boogie board
   B   prop
   C   shuttle
   D   all of the above

20. Which can fly?

   A   riband
   B   clover
   C   jackdaw
   D   applicant

© MR STEGGELS ADVANCED INSTRUCTION PTY LTD

Solutions

Unit 1

Definitions

1	fuse	5	experimental	9	skeptical	13	ballistic
2	trilogy	6	welded	10	retrieve	14	grant
3	disheartened	7	riot	11	venture	15	entranced
4	fantasy	8	humbly	12	discarded	16	foe

Word usage

1	trilogy	5	riot	9	foe	13	welded
2	fantasy	6	experimental	10	humbly	14	venture
3	ballistic	7	entranced	11	grant	15	skeptical
4	retrieve	8	disheartened	12	discarded	16	fuse

Unit 2

Definitions

1	cross	5	summon	9	extravagant	13	brooding
2	debris	6	organic	10	modern	14	fictitious
3	petrified	7	light-hearted	11	fusion	15	membership
4	barren	8	insurance	12	depicted	16	ambassador

Word usage

1	insurance	5	ambassador	9	fusion	13	cross
2	summon	6	brooding	10	debris	14	barren
3	extravagant	7	membership	11	petrified	15	modern
4	fictitious	8	light-hearted	12	organic	16	depicted

Unit 3

Definitions

1	joint	5	exquisite	9	disagreement	13	sermon
2	vile	6	boogie board	10	baste	14	paltry
3	snorkeling	7	enchanting	11	strenuous	15	squabble
4	beloved	8	befriended	12	bitter	16	doubled over

© MR STEGGELS ADVANCED INSTRUCTION PTY LTD

Unit 3

Word usage

1	bitter	5	paltry	9	boogie board	13	exquisite
2	disagreement	6	enchanting	10	strenuous	14	baste
3	doubled over	7	snorkeling	11	sermon	15	beloved
4	squabble	8	befriended	12	joint	16	vile

Unit 4

Definitions

1	herding	5	sturdy	9	immense	13	system
2	conditions	6	reckon	10	manufactured	14	specific
3	characteristics	7	activate	11	rejected	15	scrapheap
4	surrender	8	culprit	12	emission	16	services

Word usage

1	reckon	5	rejected	9	specific	13	system
2	immense	6	surrender	10	conditions	14	emission
3	scrapheap	7	characteristics	11	herding	15	activate
4	services	8	sturdy	12	culprit	16	manufactured

Unit 5

Definitions

1	animation	5	flock	9	maiden voyage	13	compact
2	anonymous	6	technology	10	scientifically	14	formula
3	belfry	7	mode	11	military	15	fantasies
4	market	8	toppling	12	hovercraft	16	electronics

Word usage

1	mode	5	market	9	belfry	13	technology
2	fantasies	6	flock	10	scientifically	14	electronics
3	hovercraft	7	anonymous	11	military	15	formula
4	maiden voyage	8	animation	12	compact	16	toppling

© MR STEGGELS ADVANCED INSTRUCTION PTY LTD

Unit 6

Definitions

1	peril	5	arduous	9	heir	13	hieroglyphs
2	routine	6	unruly	10	maternal	14	melodic
3	paternal	7	texture	11	pace	15	nuisance
4	pig-headed	8	built-in	12	truncated	16	mirage

Word usage

1	built-in	5	pig-headed	9	routine	13	peril
2	heir	6	texture	10	maternal	14	pace
3	arduous	7	melodic	11	unruly	15	hieroglyphs
4	mirage	8	paternal	12	truncated	16	nuisance

Unit 7

Definitions

1	rash	5	ratio	9	cinematography	13	conditioned
2	survey	6	tension	10	frail	14	measured
3	riband	7	occurrence	11	affect	15	taunting
4	hair-raising	8	crockery	12	anticipated	16	jackdaw

Word usage

1	measured	5	frail	9	tension	13	riband
2	ratio	6	survey	10	cinematography	14	crockery
3	conditioned	7	jackdaw	11	occurrence	15	anticipated
4	affect	8	hair-raising	12	rash	16	taunting

Unit 8

Definitions

1	apprentice	5	boycott	9	issue	13	perceptions
2	intend	6	anatomy	10	critical	14	applicant
3	refreshments	7	clover	11	representation	15	robust
4	prop	8	canal	12	superstitious	16	quiche

© MR STEGGELS ADVANCED INSTRUCTION PTY LTD

Unit 8

Word usage

1	intend	5	superstitious	9	representation	13	issue
2	refreshments	6	robust	10	boycott	14	quiche
3	prop	7	canal	11	critical	15	clover
4	anatomy	8	perceptions	12	apprentice	16	applicant

Unit 9

Definitions

1	exotic	5	shimmered	9	imitation	13	contorted
2	groundbreaking	6	separation	10	migrants	14	homeland
3	traditional	7	careering	11	introduced	15	condemned
4	benefits	8	furrowed	12	stern	16	drone

Word usage

1	drone	5	benefits	9	condemned	13	traditional
2	separation	6	furrowed	10	contorted	14	introduced
3	groundbreaking	7	imitation	11	careering	15	migrants
4	stern	8	exotic	12	shimmered	16	homeland

Unit 10

Definitions

1	breastplate	5	shuttle	9	potential	13	whereabouts
2	genuine	6	inflame	10	reviewer	14	extinguish
3	threadbare	7	truancy	11	shrill	15	praised
4	stringent	8	heroic	12	amnesty	16	prominent

Word usage

1	amnesty	5	reviewer	9	shrill	13	potential
2	praised	6	stringent	10	breastplate	14	threadbare
3	whereabouts	7	truancy	11	shuttle	15	prominent
4	genuine	8	heroic	12	inflame	16	extinguish

Test 1 solutions

Q	A	Notes
1	B	**mode** refers to a way of operating, living, or behaving; a type of something
2	A	**entranced** means cannot stop watching something or someone; captivated
3	C	**stern** and **stringent** mean serious and strict
4	D	**inflame** means to increase the intensity of a fire; **extinguish** means to put out a fire
5	C	A, B and D are occupations/jobs; an **applicant** applies for a job
6	B	Species that are **introduced** into an ecosystem often have no natural predators.
7	D	**mmnosu → summon** to increase your courage or strength, with great effort
8	A	**squabble** and **disagreement** mean a minor dispute
9	D	**imitation** means fake; **genuine** means real and exactly what appears to be
10	B	I **doubled over** when my friend fell victim to my practical joke.
11	A	**clover** is a small **green** plant with three round leaves on each stem
12	C	a **survey** is an **examination** of opinions made by asking people questions
13	A	**pig-headed** means showing unreasonable support for an opinion or plan of action and refusing to change or listen to different opinions; stubborn
14	B	**texture** is the degree to which something is rough, smooth, soft or hard, which is related to the sense of **touch**
15	D	A, B and C are verbs; **foe** is a noun
16	C	For security reasons, the **whereabouts** of pop singer Bustin Jeiber remain secret.
17	A	**odern → drone** a continuous low dull sound
18	A	**arduous** and **strenuous** describe a task or experience that is physically difficult
19	D	**tension** is mental or emotional strain
20	C	We all **anticipated** an exciting performance as the lights went down in the auditorium and the curtains open.

Test 2 solutions

Q	A	Notes
1	B	**disheartened** means lost confidence, hope, and energy
2	D	**insurance** is an agreement in which a company pays your costs if you have an accident
3	B	**robust** means strong and healthy; unlikely to break or fail **sturdy** means strong and not easily hurt or affected by what happens
4	D	**organic** means natural; **manufactured** means made goods in large quantities in a factory
5	D	**herding** is the act of moving a large number of animals, such as cattle, to another place
6	A	Customers threatened to **boycott** the company until it could prove that their products had not been tested on animals.
7	D	**tinned** → **intend** to have as a plan or purpose
8	D	**rejected** and **discarded** mean thrown away because not longer wanted or needed
9	B	**fusion** means to bring together; **separation** means to take apart
10	C	Members of the council outlined the many **benefits** that a new library would bring to the community.
11	B	Sharon worked as an **apprentice** mechanic for two years before opening her own auto repair shop.
12	A	**crockery** includes cups, plates, bowls, used to serve food and drink
13	B	**scientifically** means in a way that uses the organised methods of science
14	B	**peril** means great **danger**, or something that is very dangerous
15	C	A, B and D are nouns; **humbly** is an adverb
16	B	The **military** used advanced **technology** to locate enemy forces.
17	A	**conker** → **reckon** to believe that something is true
18	A	**melodic** means having a melody, pleasant to listen to; **shrill** means having a loud and high sound that is unpleasant to listen to
19	D	A, B and C are all subjects of study
20	C	Up ahead, I thought I saw a city rising from the desert sand, but it was just **a mirage**.

© MR STEGGELS ADVANCED INSTRUCTION PTY LTD

Test 3 solutions

Q	A	Notes
1	C	**skeptical** means doubting that something is true or useful
2	A	**grant** means to give or allow, an amount of money to be used for study or research
3	C	**ballistic** means very angry → **furious**
4	D	**anonymous** means **unknown**; **prominent** means well known, highly visible
5	C	A, B and D are verbs; **ratio** is a noun
6	D	Only the bravest of explorers would **venture** into uncharted waters.
7	B	**dweeld** → **welded** joined two pieces of metal together permanently by melting
8	C	He was **extravagant** every time he went shopping for new clothes and accessories.
9	B	The council is responsible for providing a range of **services** to the community.
10	D	Police are hoping to identify the **culprit** by using video surveillance footage.
11	C	**Membership** to my gym is quite expensive as it has a heated pool and tennis court.
12	A	**paltry** means very small and of little or no value; **extravagant** means spending too much money, or using too much of something
13	A	**debris** (broken or torn pieces of something larger) would be found on a scrapheap
14	C	**barren** means not creating or producing anything new, empty of life
15	B	**hieroglyphs** are pictures or symbols that represent a word, used in some writing systems, such as the one used in **ancient** Egypt
16	D	The go-kart went **careering** down the embankment toward the river.
17	B	**nyuurl** → **unruly** difficult to keep tidy neat, often sticking up or out
18	B	a **reviewer** is something who writes their critical opinion of a book, play, film etc
19	D	**retrieve** means to find and bring back something; **discard** means to throw away
20	A	I designed a **system** to dispatch mail quickly.

© MR STEGGELS ADVANCED INSTRUCTION PTY LTD

Test 4 solutions

Q	A	Notes
1	D	**experimental** means relating to tests, especially scientific ones
2	A	a **fantasy** is a story about situations that are very different from real life, involving magic
3	B	**enchanting** means very pleasant; **vile** means extremely unpleasant
4	C	**contorted** means **twisted** or bent in an unnatural way
5	A	**superstitious** describes someone who believes that causes for events are based old ideas about magic
6	B	When writing a recipe, it is very important to provide **specific** instructions.
7	B	**gorilty → trilogy** a series of three written about the same situation or characters, forming a continuous story
8	C	The general will lead a **campaign** to take control of enemy states by force.
9	D	A, B and C are all foods.
10	C	**squabbling** is arguing over something that is not important
11	C	**Careering** down a steep hill on skis is a **hair-raising** experience.
12	D	**traditional** means being part of the unchanging customs of a group of people or ways of behaving; **modern** means belonging to the present
13	B	a **hovercraft** is a vehicle that travels quickly just above the surface of water or land by producing a current of air under it to support it; a **boogie board** is a piece of sporting/leisure equipment
14	D	There was **a formula** for making his fried chicken that Colonel Flanders wanted kept secret.
15	A	**praised** means expressed admiration or approval about the achievements or characteristics of a person or thing; **condemned** means disapproved of completely
16	B	Eastville did not agree to the **conditions** of **surrender** so Westville decided to end the war by dropping a nuclear bomb.
17	A	**choire → heroic** very brave or great
18	C	**snorkeling** is swimming while using a tube that you hold in your mouth to help you breathe with your face underwater
19	D	an **issue** is a subject that people are thinking and talking about
20	C	The **ratio** of flour to sugar is two to one.

Test 5 solutions

Q	A	Notes
1	B	**depicted** means represented or shown something in a picture or story
2	D	**exquisite** means very beautiful and delicate
3	C	**truncated** means made briefer or shorter, usually by removing a part
4	A	**rash** means careless or unwise, without thought for what might happen; **measured** means careful and controlled
5	C	A, B and D are nouns; **activate** is a verb
6	B	The **migrants** escaped their **homeland** when war broke out.
7	C	etcaff → **affect** to have an influence on someone or something, or to cause a change
8	D	A look of concern **furrowed** my mother's forehead when she learned that I had stolen my brother's pocket money.
9	A	The designer kitchen featured a **built-in** butler's pantry with a secret door.
10	B	**market** means the part of the economy where products and services are sold
11	C	**flock** (verb) to move or come together in large numbers **flock** (noun) a large number of animals
12	A	**foe** means an enemy; **beloved** means someone who or something that is loved very much
13	D	**fantasies** refers to pleasant situations that you enjoy thinking about but which are unlikely to happen
14	C	a **canal** a long, thin stretch of water that is artificially made for boats to travel along
15	B	**immense** means extremely large; **compact** means consisting of parts that are positioned closely or in a tidy way, using very little space
16	B	The cladding on the tower is a **potential** fire hazard and should be removed.
17	D	**simonies** → **emission** a substance, especially a gas, released into the air
18	A	**brooding** means sad, worried, or angry for a long time; **light-hearted** means happy and not serious
19	D	**boogie board** (verb) a short, light board that you lie on and ride over waves (noun) the act of riding on such a board **prop** (verb) to support something physically, often by leaning it against something else or putting something under it (noun) an item used in a performance **shuttle** (verb) travel regularly between two places (noun) a vehicle used for this purpose
20	C	a **jackdaw** is a black and grey bird of the crow family, known for taking bright objects back to its nest

© MR STEGGELS ADVANCED INSTRUCTION PTY LTD

www.ingramcontent.com/pod-product-compliance
Lightning Source LLC
LaVergne TN
LVHW061318060426
835507LV00019B/2215